MAKING AND BREAKING CODES

BREAKING SECRET CODES

BY JILLIAN GREGORY

Consultant:
Professor Mihir Bellare
Department of Computer Science and Engineering
University of California, San Diego

CAPSTONE PRESS
a capstone imprint

Edge Books are published by Capstone Press,
151 Good Counsel Drive, P.O. Box 669, Mankato, Minnesota 56002.
www.capstonepub.com

Library of Congress Cataloging-in-Publication Data
Gregory, Jillian.
  Breaking secret codes / by Jillian Gregory.
    p. cm.—(Making and breaking codes)
  Includes bibliographical references and index.
  Summary: "Discusses different methods for breaking secret codes"—Provided
    by publisher.
  ISBN 978-1-4296-4568-3 (library binding)
  1. Cryptography—Juvenile literature. 2. Ciphers—Juvenile literature. I. Title.
  Z103.3G737 2011
  652'.8—dc22   2010004162

1207

EDITORIAL CREDITS

Mandy Robbins, editor; Ted Williams, designer; Marcie Spence,
    media researcher; Laura Manthe, production specialist

PHOTO CREDITS

Alamy/Photos 12, 24; Alamy/Photo Researchers, 28; Bob Thomas/
Popperfoto/Getty Images Inc., 5; Capstone Press/Karon Dubke 10, 11, 13;
Hulton Archive/Getty Images Inc., 4; Library of Congress, 7; Newscom,
14 (top), 19, 23; Newscom/AFP Photo/Karen Bleier, 16; Shutterstock/
Adrio Communications Ltd., cover, 14 (bottom); Shutterstock/c., 8;
Shutterstock/Christophe Testi, 21; Shutterstock/Ingvald Kaldhussater, 27;
Shutterstock/markhiggins, 17; Shutterstock/Shotgun, 9

Printed in the United States of America in Stevens Point, Wisconsin.
022011   006090R

TABLE OF CONTENTS

THE QUEEN'S CODE CRACKERS

In the mid-1500s, Mary, Queen of Scots, was planning to kill her cousin, Queen Elizabeth. In doing so, Mary could take over the English throne. But Elizabeth didn't trust Mary and was holding her prisoner. Mary had many supporters, though. She exchanged letters with them written in a secret code. These letters contained plans to kill Elizabeth.

But Mary soon learned the value of a secure code. Queen Elizabeth's supporters got hold of Mary's letters and cracked the code. Mary's punishment for her plot was death.

Queen Elizabeth ruled England from 1558 to 1603.

Mary, Queen of Scots, denied being involved in the plot to kill Queen Elizabeth.

TRACKING DOWN CLUES

Code breakers try to **decode** a message without knowing the **key**. Their knowledge of code-making techniques helps them break codes. Patterns in the coded text can give clues about how to crack it.

Anyone can be a code breaker, including you. By the time you finish reading this book, you should be able to decode the message below.

WUDYKI YI EDU FUHSUDJ YDIFYHQJYED QDT DYDUJO DYDU FUHSUDJ FUHIFYHQJYED.

decode—to turn something that is written in code into ordinary language

key—the process by which information is encoded and decoded

TRANSPOSITION CODES

Secret codes have changed the course of history. Written and spoken codes have helped military leaders win wars. Prisoners of war used tap codes to communicate with each other. Today, complex computer codes protect personal information online. However, every code can be cracked by figuring out the key.

One simple code method is **transposition**. This method mixes up letters, numbers, or symbols to **encode** a message. Transposition could be as simple as writing a message backward. Letters may also be jumbled up within the words themselves. Or the entire message could be mixed up.

transposition—to rearrange the order of items in something
encode—to turn something that is written in ordinary language into coded text

CODE FACT

The Union Route code was a transposition code used by Union forces during the Civil War (1861–1865). Officers sent messages from telegraph stations set up near battlefields.

MIRROR WRITING

In the 1500s, Leonardo daVinci used an odd form of transposition in his journals. He wrote backward from right to left. His writing could only be read if it was held up to a mirror. Some people think this was a simple way for daVinci to disguise his scientific findings. Other people think daVinci used mirror writing because he was left-handed. In the 1500s, people used feathers dipped in ink to write. A left-handed person writing from left to right would smear ink across the page. Writing backward kept daVinci's writing from getting smudged!

When faced with decoding a message, first assume it's a simple transposition. See if you can rearrange the letters to make sense. If you can't, move on to a trickier code-cracking technique.

The following three lines are transpositions of the same phrase. The first line is the most difficult to crack. The second and third lines get easier.

1. fa lboslr fga ierte
2. retag lsbla fo irfe
3. erif fo sllab taerg

☑ *See page 32 for answer.*

GEOMETRIC CODES

Sometimes coded messages are transposed using a grid. A geometric code takes a message in plain text and rearranges it in a grid. When a message is presented as equal groups of characters, it was probably created with a geometric code. Even if one or two groups are shorter than the others, it may still be a geometric code. The odd groupings are probably caused by a partially empty last column. If the message didn't fit perfectly into the grid, the last column would have empty squares.

The key to cracking a geometric code is to figure out the size of the grid. This is not as tricky as it may seem. The number of columns is equal to the number of letters in each word group of the coded message. The number of rows in the grid is equal to the total number of word groups in the message. Once you've made your grid, plug in the letters. The final trick is figuring out which way to read the grid.

The coded message fits into a four-row by five-column grid. Follow the arrows to read the secret message.

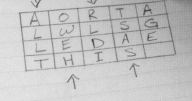

✓ See page 32 for answer.

DO IT YOURSELF!

Using what you've learned about geometric codes, see if you can decode this message:

TLA HEN EHD EAE ASD GL

☑ *See page 32 for answer.*

Most of the groupings are the same length. This suggests the message was written using a geometric code. Most groups have three letters. That means your grid needs three columns. There are six groups of coded text. Give your grid six rows. Write the message in the grid. Look for real words to figure out which direction to read the grid.

T	L	A
H	E	N
E	H	D
E	A	E
A	S	D
G	L	

CODE FACT

Geometric codes can be created using many shapes. A pyramid-shaped grid would create a message that started with one letter. The letter groupings would grow by one letter with each group.

To make geometric codes trickier, the message may be written in a confusing order. A four by four grid may read up the first column and then down the third column. Then it may read up the fourth, and down the second column.

See if you can create a grid to decode this message. Then figure out what order to read it in.

?OWECC ROHHEO AKOTHO JIPNTK EEUITI

☑ *See page 32 for answer.*

CHAPTER 2

SUBSTITUTION CODES

Samuel Morse invented Morse code to be used with the telegraph.

Another common type of key is the substitution method. Substitution replaces letters in the message with new letters, symbols, or numbers.

A codebook can contain the key to breaking a substitution code. The codebook shows the meaning of each part of the code.

MORSE CODE

One commonly used substitution code is Morse code. Morse code replaces each number and letter with a series of dots and dashes. Use the Morse code key to decode the following message:

... .- -- .. .-. . .-..   -- --- .-. ... .

.. -. ...- . -. - . -..   -- --- .-. ... .

-.-. --- -.. . .. -. .---- --.. ....- ....-

MORSE CODE KEY

A .–	J .– – –	S ...	2 ..– – –
B –...	K –.–	T –	3 ...– –
C –.–.	L .–..	U ..–	4 ....–
D –..	M – –	V ...–	5 .....
E .	N –.	W .– –	6 –....
F ..–.	O – – –	X –..–	7 – –...
G – –.	P .– –.	Y –.– –	8 – – –..
H	Q – –.–	Z – –..	9 – – – –.
I ..	R .–.	1 .– – – –	0 – – – – –

✓ *See page 32 for answer.*

PHONE CODE

If you text message, you probably crack codes every day. People who text message often use a shorthand substitution code. This code replaces whole words or phrases with letters. BRB means, "be right back." TTYL means "talk to you later."

Emoticons are used to show emotion in a text message. A winking smiley face means you are joking. For those who don't know them, these codes are easy enough to crack. Text message and emoticon codebooks can be found on the Internet.

emoticon—a group of letters or punctuation symbols that represents facial expressions and emotion

CRACKING THE ENIGMA

During World War II (1939–1945), the German military encoded messages using the Enigma machine. The machine replaced each letter of text with a random letter found on 26 rotating wheels. Because the wheels rotated, a different code letter was used each time a letter was typed. If the letter E was used five times, five different letters could replace it. Encoded messages were sent in Morse code by a telegraph operator. A person needed more than another Enigma machine to decode a message. He also needed to know what key settings to use.

British code-breaker Alan Turing led a team that developed a machine called the Colossus. Colossus could crack the Enigma code. Much of Turing's research became the basis for building modern-day computers. Turing is often called the father of computer science.

FREQUENCY ANALYSIS

But what if you don't know the key? How do you decode a secret message? When there are double letters in a coded message, it's likely a substitution code was used. Substitution codes can be cracked using a technique called frequency analysis. This technique uses common patterns in the English language to crack codes.

Use the following tips to help you break codes using frequency analysis.

1. The 26 letters of the English alphabet from most commonly used to least commonly used are: E, T, A, O, I, N, S, R, H, L, D, C, U, M, F, P, G, W, Y, B, V, K, X, Q, J, Z.

2. The only one-letter words are "I" and "A."

3. The most common three-letter words are "and" and "the."

4. The most common double letters are "ss," "ll," "ee," "nn," "tt," "ff," "cc," "rr," "mm," and "pp."

Use these tips to crack this secret message:

LZW CWWF WQW KWWK SDD.

☑ *See page 32 for answer.*

Need a little help? Turn the page for step-by-step instructions.

CODE FACT

In 1839, author Edgar Allen Poe challenged readers of *Alexander's Weekly Messenger* to submit substitution codes. He solved 99 out of the 100 codes submitted to the challenge.

STEP-BY-STEP CRACKING

When cracking a substitution code, begin by writing the coded message on a piece of paper. Leave room below the message to write in the real text as you crack it. Use a pencil so you can erase any unsuccessful attempts.

Your next step is to make a frequency chart. To do this, write the letters of the alphabet in the first row. Then count the number of times each letter appears in the secret message. For example, there is one L in the message. Record this information in the second row of the chart.

A	B	C	D	E	F	G	H	I	J	K	L	M
		1	2		1					2	1	

N	O	P	Q	R	S	T	U	V	W	X	Y	Z
			1		1				7			1

The most frequent letter in the secret message is W. Using the frequency list, W most likely represents the letter E. The next most common letters in the coded text are K and D. Substitute T for K and A for D. This substitution creates "TEET" and "_AA." Those are not real words. Continue to use the letters in the frequency list until real words appear. In this case, K stands for S and D means L.

CODED TEXT	LZW	CWWF	WQW	KWWK	SDD
PLAIN TEXT	_ _ E	_ E E _	E _ E	SEES	_ LL

Also look for real-word clues in the secret message. What three-letter words begin and end with E?

Once a few letters of plain text have been solved, create a chart of the alphabet. Plug in the letters you know. Substitution codes often shift the entire alphabet a certain number of spaces. See if you can fill in the rest of the alphabet in order.

PLAIN TEXT	A	B	C	D	E	F	G	H	I	J	K	L	M
CODE TEXT				L								S	

PLAIN TEXT	N	O	P	Q	R	S	T	U	V	W	X	Y	Z
CODE TEXT				Y						E			

The key to the code is shown below.

A	B	C	D	E	F	G	H	I	J	K	L	M
I	J	K	L	M	N	O	P	Q	R	S	T	U

N	O	P	Q	R	S	T	U	V	W	X	Y	Z
V	W	X	Y	Z	A	B	C	D	E	F	G	H

Now try to decode two more messages on your own.

1. **NLCWE IL NLYUN MGYFF GS ZYYN**
2. **T EPGGV BTYPQ LB T EPGGV PTCGPQ**

☑ *See page 32 for answers.*

REBEL HACKER

James Lovell was an American **cryptologist** during the Revolutionary War (1775–1783). Lovell was on the Committee for Foreign Affairs. He cracked coded messages stolen from British commander Lord Cornwallis. One message revealed that Cornwallis was waiting in Yorktown for more British troops. The Americans used this information to force Lord Cornwallis to surrender.

cryptologist—a person who studies the science of

BOOK CIPHERS AND BEYOND

In the movie *National Treasure*, treasure hunters break secret codes created by America's founding fathers.

In the movie *National Treasure*, treasure hunters try to break codes that lead to a hidden treasure. They find a code on the back of the Declaration of Independence called an Ottendorf **cipher**. Discovering the key will lead them closer to the treasure. The Ottendorf cipher is an example of a book cipher.

Book ciphers are codes that use an outside source as a key. In *National Treasure*, the key texts were letters written by Benjamin Franklin. Common books like *Merriam-Webster's Dictionary* and the Bible are often used as keys to book ciphers as well. Book ciphers are usually presented as a series of numbers. Hyphens often separate the numbers. The numbers refer to a letter or word in the key text. For example 3-7-4 could represent the fourth word on the seventh line of the third page of a book.

cipher—a system used to send secret messages; another word for a code

SOLVE THE CIPHER

A book cipher is impossible to break unless you know what the key text is. Even when you do, there is some guesswork involved. You have to figure out what the numbers stand for. Do they lead you to a page number or a chapter number? Does the final number represent a letter or an entire word?

Using what you've learned about book ciphers, try to decode this message:

4–5–3

6–7–1

15–5–1

14–9–2

☑ *See page 32 for answer.*

Having a little trouble? Here's a hint: The key is in your hands.

BEATING COMPUTER HACKERS

When people buy something over the Internet, they pay with a credit card. Their credit card information streams over the Internet. Hackers have programs that pick up information being sent over the Internet. These programs help hackers steal credit card information. To prevent theft, credit card information is encoded by a computer system before being sent over the Internet. This computer system is called Secure Sockets Layer (SSL). SSL uses public-key cryptography, which uses two different keys. Information is encoded by the shopper's computer with the store's public key. The information is decoded by the store using an associated private key.

Public-key cryptography improves upon past codes that were encoded and decoded with the same key. To crack public-key cryptography, you need to quickly **factor** very large numbers. The largest number ever cracked was about 200 digits. Cryptographers create codes with numbers of 300 or more digits for safety.

factor—to find numbers that are multiplied together to form a result; for example, 5 and 17 are factors of 85 because 5 times 17 equals 85

CHAPTER 4

WHAT WAS THE SECRET MESSAGE?

As long as people have been creating codes, others have been trying to crack them. There are many tips that can help you crack codes. But trial and error is a big part of it.

In Chapter One you were given a secret message. You don't have to be a genius like Albert Einstein to figure it out. The tools to decode this message are now in your hands. In fact, there's even a clue in this paragraph about who said it.

✓ *See page 32 for answer.*

Famous scientist Albert Einstein developed the theory of relativity.

KEEP CRACKING!

Do you want to try cracking even more codes? See if you can decode the following fun facts about codes using tips you learned in this book.

1. PDA AJECIW IWYDEJA SWO EJRAJPAZ EJ 1915

2. - .... .   .-. --- -. --. . ... -

-- --- .-. ... .   -.-. --- -.. .   -- . ...- --. .

. ...- . .-.   ... . -. -   .-- .- ... .   - .... .

-. . ...- .- -.- .-   -.-. --- -. ... .. -.. . .-. .. --- -.

3. ITFCTEN PHFLERE HOEEDSV EMJEAON RASHWNI

☑ *See page 32 for answers.*

CODE FACT

Modern cryptographers are focusing on a complex technique called quantum cryptography. This type of code can't be cracked without the hacker leaving evidence behind.

INDEX

☑ ANSWERS

PAGE 5: *Genius is one percent inspiration and ninety-nine percent perspiration.*

PAGE 9: *great balls of fire*

PAGE 11: *All the world is a stage.*

PAGE 12: *The eagle has landed.*

PAGE 13: *Who put the cookie in the cookie jar?*

PAGE 15: *Samuel Morse invented Morse code in 1844.*

PAGE 19: *The keen eye sees all.*

PAGE 23:
1. *Trick or treat. Smell my feet.*
2. *A penny saved is a penny earned.*

PAGE 26: *Mary cracked the code.*

PAGE 29:
1. *The Enigma machine was invented in 1915.*
2. *The longest Morse Code message ever sent was the Nevada Constitution.*
3. *Thomas Jefferson invented a wheel cipher.*